THE BIG PICTURE

STORY BIBLE

PRESENTED TO

_____

FROM

_____

DATE

_____

In memory of
Daniel Mark Oster
May 29–31, 1997

Download a free audio reading by
the author at www.bigpicturestorybible.com.

THE BIG PICTURE

STORY BIBLE

Written by David R. Helm

Illustrations by Gail Schoonmaker

:: CROSSWAY®

WHEATON, ILLINOIS

The Big Picture Story Bible

Text copyright © 2004 by Holy Trinity Church

Illustrations copyright © by Gail Schoonmaker

Published by Crossway
       1300 Crescent Street
       Wheaton, Illinois 60187

Cover illustration: Gail Schoonmaker

First edition 2004

Second edition with audio 2010

Reprinted with new cover 2014

Printed in China

Hardcover ISBN: 978-1-4335-4311-1

ePub ISBN: 978-1-4335-3148-4

Mobipocket ISBN: 978-1-4335-3544-4

Library of Congress Cataloging-in-Publication Data

Helm, David R., 1961-
    The big picture story Bible / David Helm ; illustrations by Gail Schoonmaker.
      p. cm.
    ISBN 13: 978-1-58134-277-2 (hardcover : alk. paper)
    ISBN 10: 1-58134-277-2
    1. Bible stories, English. I. Schoonmaker, Gail. II. Title.
BS551.3.H45 2004
220.9'505--dc22   2004006561

Crossway is a publishing ministry of Good News Publishers.

RRDS	30	29	28	27	26	25	24	23	22	21
21	20	19	18	17	16	15	14	13	12	11	10	9	8

For my children—
Noah, Joanna, Baxter, Silas, and Mariah,
and the children of their generation,
that they may come to know by faith
what Daniel already knows by sight.
D. H.

For my parents,
who introduced me to the forever king
and taught me to love his holy book,
that their faithful labor for the kingdom
may continue to bear fruit in coming generations.
G. S.

Contents

Acknowledgments 13

The Old Testament

Part 1   The Very Good Beginning 15

Part 2   A Very Sad Day 37

Part 3   Life outside the Garden 51

Part 4   God's Big Promise 67

Part 5   God's People Grow 83

Part 6   God's People Become Great 103

Part 7   God's Great Sign 123

Part 8   Going into God's Place 141

Part 9   God's Blessings Grow 167

Part 10   Another Very Sad Day 187

Part 11   God's Promise Remains 211

The New Testament

Part 12   Many Silent Years 229

Part 13   God's Promised One Is Born 243

Part 14   God's Promised One Is Announced.... 259

Part 15   God's New People Are Called............. 271

Part 16   Jesus Restores God's Place 287

Part 17   Jesus Reveals God's Kingdom 307

Part 18   A Blind Man Sees 323

Part 19   A Dead Man Is Raised to Life 337

Part 20   Jesus Wears God's Kingly Crown.........359

Part 21   Jesus's Followers Are in the Dark........ 375

Part 22   A Brand-New Day.................................... 383

Part 23   God's Promise Is Explained................... 397

Part 24   God's New Kingdom Spreads.............. 413

Part 25   Letters to Live By 427

Part 26   The Very Good Ending............................437

ACKNOWLEDGMENTS

We wish to thank Lane Dennis for his unfailing commitment to this book. The development of this project and its manuscript are enhanced thanks to the keen editing of Lila Bishop and the attention of the entire Crossway Books team. The artwork owes much to the invaluable insights of David LaPlaca. Thank you for your generous involvement, thoughtful suggestions, and endless encouragement. Further, we are indebted to Graeme Goldsworthy, who first helped us grasp the Bible along the lines of "God's people in God's place under God's rule." To the myriad friends and family whose assistance and encouragement spurred us on, thank you. Among them, Stephanie, Lanelle, Amanda, and Elda, who each baby-sat for hundreds of hours so that Gail could paint. Finally, we especially thank God for our spouses, Lisa and Keith. Without your vital support and encouragement we would have faltered long ago.

THE OLD TESTAMENT

THE VERY GOOD BEGINNING

Part 1

The Bible is God's story,
and it begins with these big words:

In the begin

"In the beginning,
God created the heavens and the earth."

17

Do you know how God created everything?

Simply by speaking words.
Imagine, making the world with words!
Strong words.
Powerful words.

With words
God created everything!
He made the stars,
the sun, and the moon.
He made the animals,
the fish, the trees, and flowers too.
Everything!

And then after all these
things, God created . . .

People!

Can you see Adam and Eve?

God put his people in the garden of Eden.
They were made in the image of God.
They were to be the rulers of God's place.

Adam and Eve were very special to God.
Did you know that you are also very special to God?
You are special because you are made in his image too!

Being created in the image of God must have
made Adam and Eve very, very happy.

God was happy too.

He was pleased with his world and his people because he saw that they were very good.

Nothing was wrong.
Nothing was bad.
Nobody disobeyed God.

29

In the very good beginning,
everything and
everyone
knew how good God was.

God gave Adam and Eve good words to obey.
He told them not to eat from a special tree.
You see, God was teaching Adam and Eve
that he was their king,
that people were to obey God's word.

God also said that
if Adam and Eve disobeyed his word,
they would surely die.

34

So God's people, Adam and Eve,
lived in God's place, the garden of Eden.
And they ruled God's world
by obeying his good word.

Do you know
what happened
next?

A VERY SAD DAY

Part 2

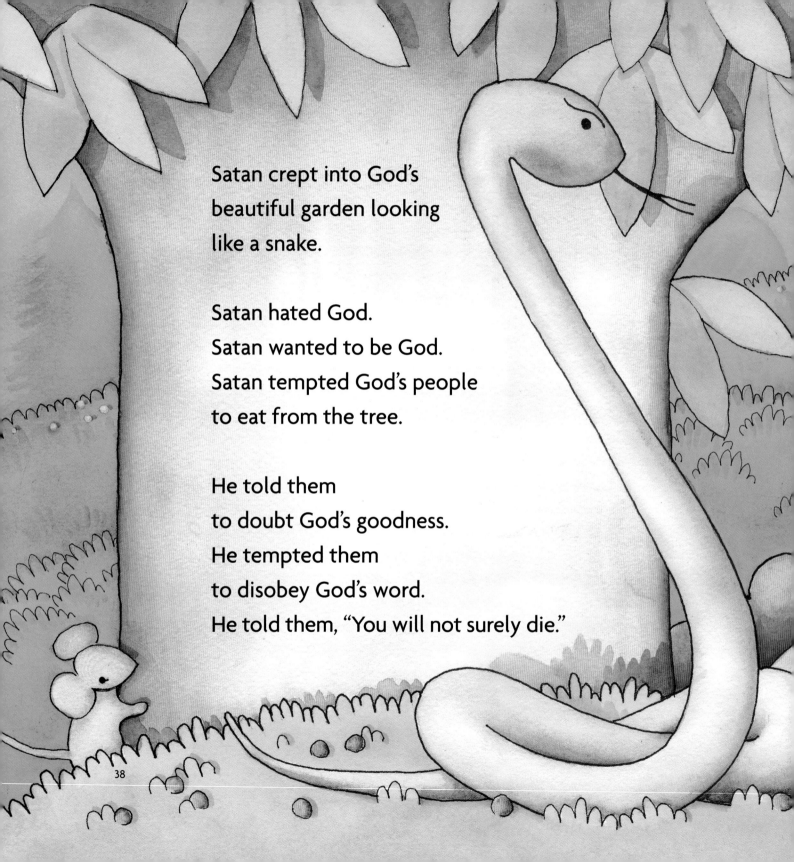

Satan crept into God's
beautiful garden looking
like a snake.

Satan hated God.
Satan wanted to be God.
Satan tempted God's people
to eat from the tree.

He told them
to doubt God's goodness.
He tempted them
to disobey God's word.
He told them, "You will not surely die."

40

Now Adam and Eve had a choice to make.
They could obey God's word,
or they could listen to Satan.

What do you think you
would have done?
Do you know what
Adam and Eve did?

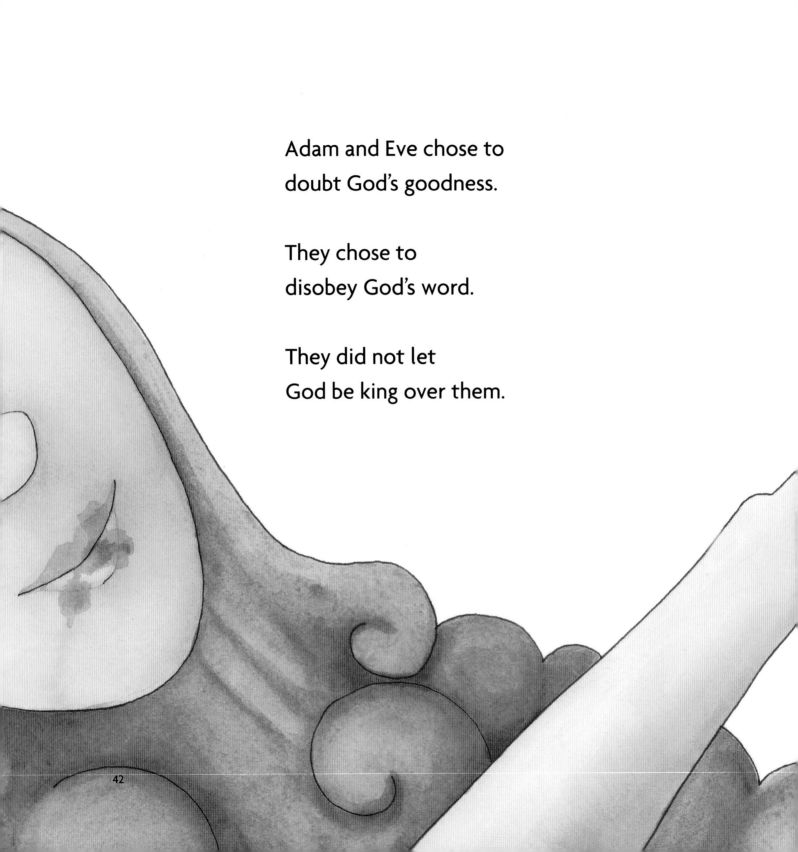

Adam and Eve chose to
doubt God's goodness.

They chose to
disobey God's word.

They did not let
God be king over them.

They ate some fruit from the tree.

They listened to the voice of Satan instead of the word of God.

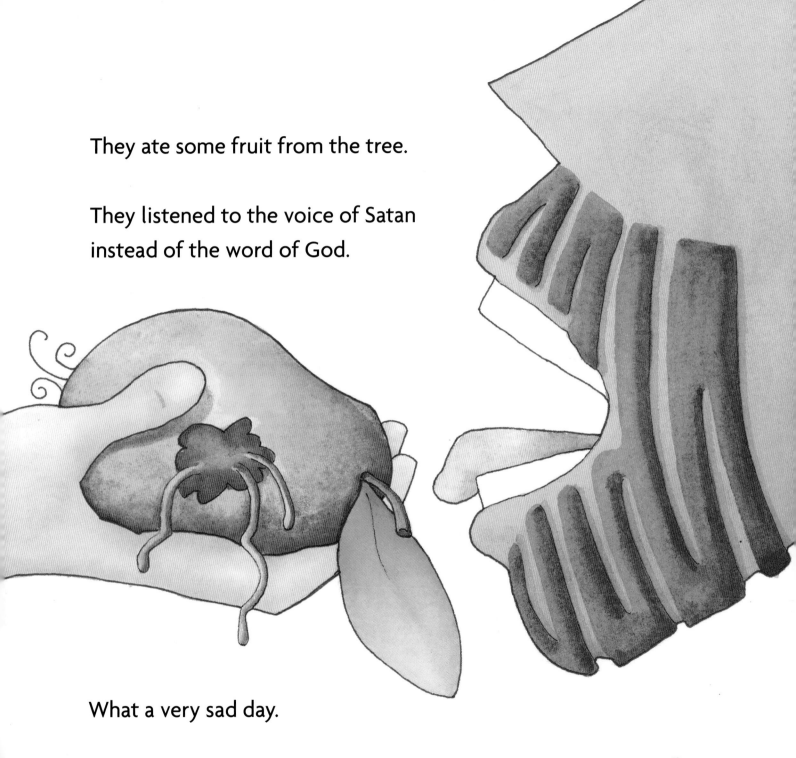

What a very sad day.

Can you imagine what God
thought about all this?

God was very angry.

44

God cursed the snake.
God punished Eve.
And God punished Adam too.

Do you know why God had to punish them?

45

God punished them because
they disobeyed God's word,
which was meant to rule
over his place and his people.

Did you know that some good news
came on this sad day too?

God gave Adam and Eve a hint
that he would not always be angry with them.

God promised that one day someone would
come and crush Satan's power over people.

But that day was a long way off.
On this very sad day,
God made Adam and Eve leave the garden.

LIFE OUTSIDE THE GARDEN

Part 3

Do you remember why God's people
had to leave God's place?

God drove Adam and Eve out of the
garden of Eden
because they disobeyed him and
rejected him as king.

And everything God had warned them
about disobeying his word came true.

Adam and Eve were now separated from God
and began having difficulty with each other.
Raising children was hard.
Finding food was even harder.
And their coming death was now beginning
to make their bodies grow older.

Life outside the garden was terrible.

Now Adam and Eve ruled the world in evil ways.
And they had children who did just the same.

Their children,
and grandchildren,
and great-grandchildren all turned away from God.

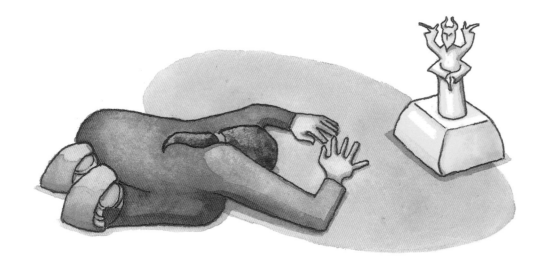

Outside the garden
everyone doubted how good God was.

Outside the garden
everyone disobeyed God's word.

Outside the garden
everyone ruled the world in evil ways.

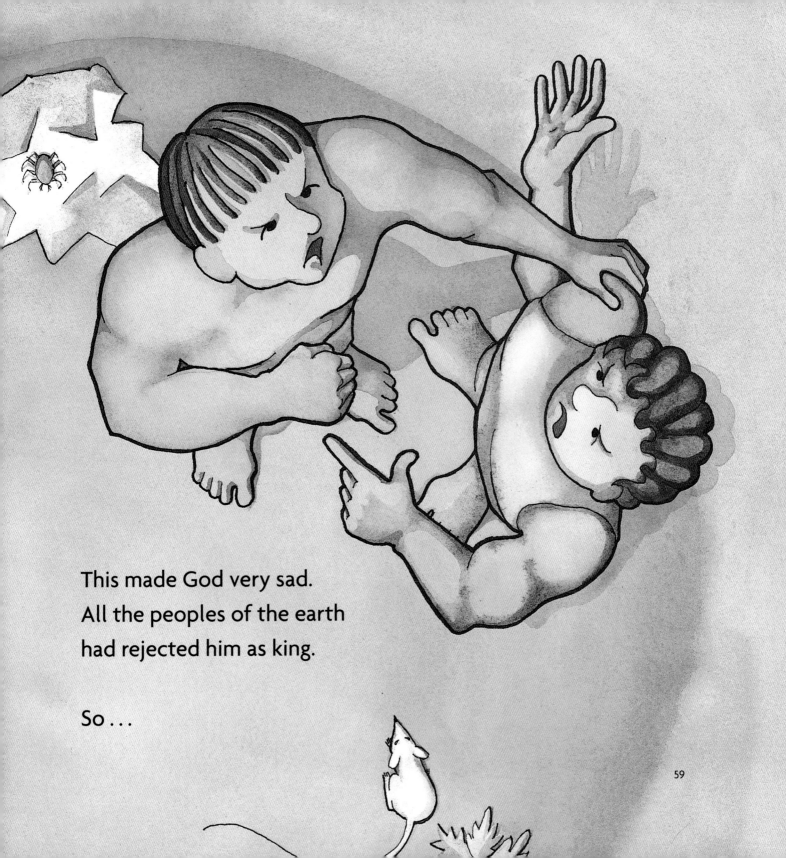

This made God very sad.
All the peoples of the earth
had rejected him as king.

So . . .

God decided to judge all the peoples of the earth.
He decided to send a big flood on the place he had made.

But there was one man, named Noah, who listened to God.
God told Noah to build a great big boat.

God told Noah to put many animals on the boat.
God told Noah to bring his family on the boat.

And Noah did what God said.

Then . . .

God judged the world.
God sent a big flood of water.
Everything that lived on land died.

But Noah, his family,
and the animals on the boat were saved.

Do you know what the flood teaches us?
God will judge every single person
who rejects him as king.

And do you know what God's judgment
teaches us?
Every single person needs God's blessing.

And guess what?
God promised to do just that!
God promised to bless all the
peoples of the earth!

GOD'S BIG PROMISE

Part 4

Many years after the flood
God made a big promise.
He said to a man named Abraham,

"Go . . . to the land I will show you.
And I will make of you a great nation. . . .
and in you all the families of the earth
shall be blessed."

69

Wow! That was good news.
God told Abraham to go to a *new place*,
because God was going to make a *new people*,
so that God's blessing would spread to *all people!*

What a big
promise God
made to Abraham!

Abraham listened to God's word,
and then Abraham did what God said.
Abraham went to the land God showed him.

Do you know how Abraham felt when he got there?

73

Abraham felt afraid.
He wasn't sure how God would keep his promise.

After all, Abraham and his wife, Sarah, were very old,
too old to have children!

One night Abraham thought and thought.
How could he become a great people
if he didn't have even one child?
And how could he become a blessing to all peoples
without children and grandchildren of his own?

God knew what Abraham was thinking.
God talked to him:
"Don't be afraid, Abraham.
Come outside and look up into the night sky.
Count all the stars, if you can. You will have
as many children as there are stars in the sky!"

So Abraham went outside.
Abraham looked up into the night sky
and tried to count the stars.

And then something happened.
As he stood there counting, suddenly . . .

Abraham believed God's word!

That made God very happy. His promise was very big,
and Abraham's faith in God's promise was very big too.

GOD'S PEOPLE GROW

Part 5

At last it happened.

God kept his promise to Abraham and gave him a son, Isaac.

God's promise of a new people was beginning to grow!

And so God's promise passed on from Abraham to Isaac.

When Isaac grew up, God gave him a son, Jacob.

God's promise was beginning to grow and grow!

And so God's promise passed on from Abraham to Isaac to Jacob.

When Jacob grew up
God gave him twelve sons!
And he named them Reuben,
Simeon, Levi, Judah, Zebulun,
Issachar, Dan, Gad, Asher,
Naphtali, Joseph,
and Benjamin.

God's promise was beginning
to grow and grow and grow!!!
But while God's people were
growing in number . . .

They also were growing apart.

Jacob's many sons hated their younger brother Joseph.
They did an evil thing.
They put him in a pit and then sold him
to be a slave in a faraway place.

Isn't that sad?
Do you think Joseph was all
alone in faraway Egypt?

No. He was not alone.

God was with Joseph.
And God was going to use this evil thing
that happened to Joseph for good!

God showed Joseph that in a few years
there wouldn't be enough food
for all the hungry people in the land.
Joseph believed God.

And Pharaoh, the king of Egypt, believed Joseph.
He put Joseph in charge of the kingdom,
and Joseph helped him by storing up food.

Then came the time of trouble, just as God had said.
People came from distant lands to buy the stored food.
They were hungry and about to die.

94

When Joseph's father Jacob
heard that there was food
in Egypt . . .

95

He told his sons to go and buy some.
So they went.

And Joseph,
now a very powerful man, recognized them.
But his brothers did not recognize Joseph.

97

After all these years,
Joseph could have gotten even with them.
Joseph could have sold them as slaves.
Joseph could have killed them.

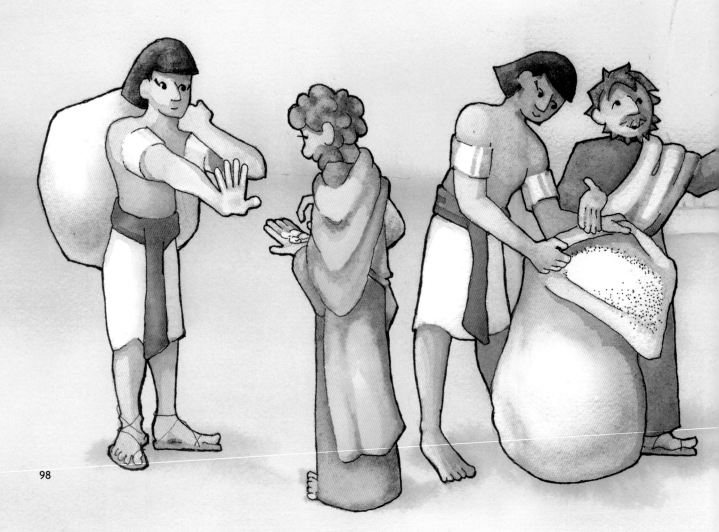

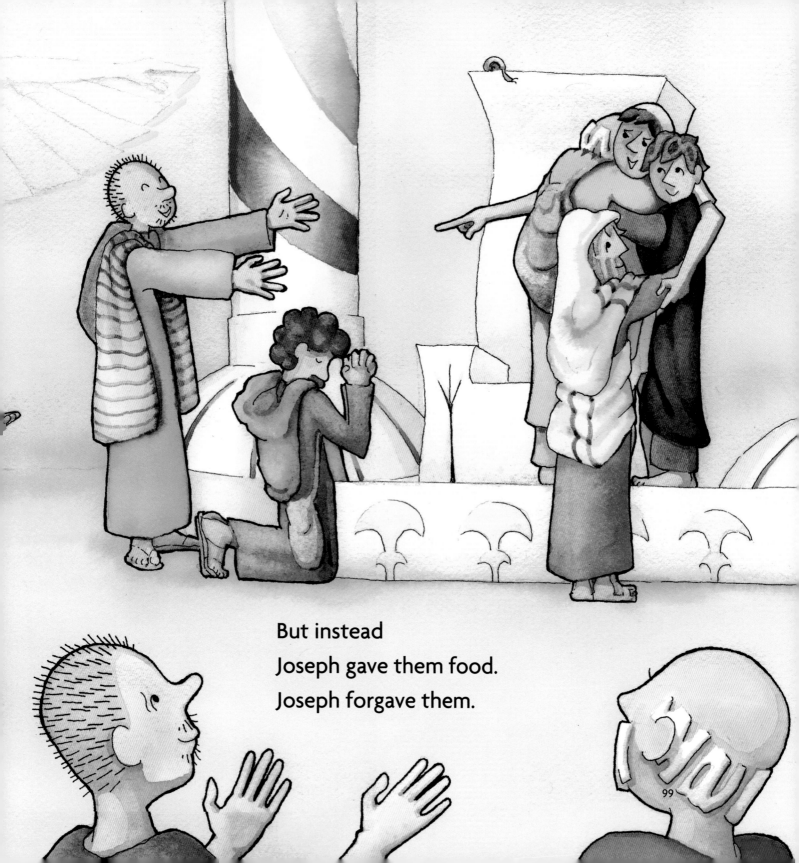

But instead
Joseph gave them food.
Joseph forgave them.

99

He told them not to worry.

He told them God had been with him in Egypt.

He told them God had sent him ahead to Egypt
so that God's people would not die.

Soon Jacob's family would begin to grow in Egypt.

GOD'S PEOPLE BECOME GREAT

Part 6

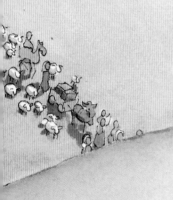

Jacob moved his growing household to Egypt.

Bags were packed.
Camels and donkeys were loaded with things,
and everyone started out.

First came Jacob, the son of Isaac,
the grandson of Abraham.
Next came Jacob's sons.
And then came all their families.
Seventy people moved to Egypt!
By now God's promise of a great people was
really growing!

And God's promise kept growing long after
Jacob and his sons died. After four hundred
years in Egypt, God's people had grown into
a great nation named Israel.

In fact, Israel had so many people
that the land was filled with them.

Do you think the Egyptians
liked having all these people in their land?

107

Pharaoh, the king of the land,
hated the people of Israel.
Pharaoh hated Israel's God too.

So he treated God's people like slaves.
He made them work, work, work.

He was so evil
that he even killed some of God's people.

109

God's people were in trouble.
They cried out to God for help,
and God heard them.

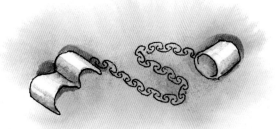

Do you see the little baby boy?
He was God's answer to the people's cry for help.
His name was Moses, and one day he would rescue
God's people.

When Moses grew up, God spoke to him.
Moses listened to God and then . . .

Moses did what God told him to do.

He went to Pharaoh and said God's words:
"Let my people go!"
But the king said no.
He did not listen to God.

Moses told Pharaoh that if he disobeyed

God's word,
terrible things would happen
to the Egyptians.

Did that make the king decide
to listen to God?
No, Pharaoh still refused to let
God's people go.

So God made
the river turn to blood.

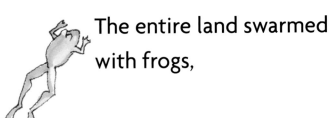 The entire land swarmed
with frogs,

But Pharaoh still refused to let God's people go.

and dust turned into gnats.

So God made
the houses full of flies.

The animals of Egypt got
sick and died,

But Pharaoh still refused to let God's people go.

and the people got painful sores.

119

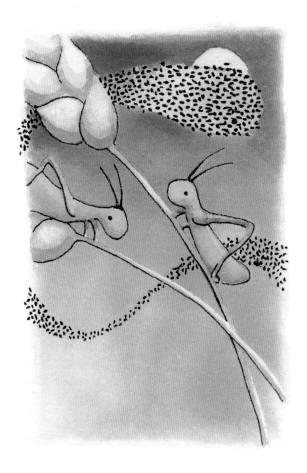

So God made
hail fall from the sky.

Locusts covered the
ground,

But Pharaoh still refused to let God's people go.

Can you imagine what it would take for Pharaoh to let God's people go?

and darkness spread out over the land.

GOD'S GREAT SIGN

Part 7

God gave Moses a message for his people.
Moses told God's people to take lambs and sacrifice them.

He told them to put the blood over their front doors.
The blood of the lamb was God's great sign.

That night the Lord took
the lives of the firstborn in homes
that did not have God's great sign.
Many Egyptians died that night.

But the Lord did not take
the lives of the firstborn in homes
that had blood over their doors.
God "passed over" the families of Israel.

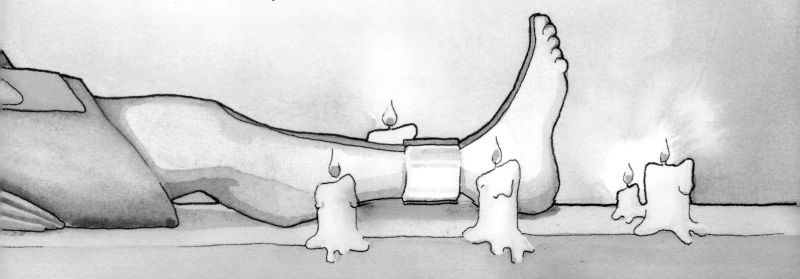

At last Pharaoh stopped
pretending to be God.
He listened to God and
told God's people, "Go!"

Can you see the grandpas and grandmas,
the men and women,
the children and grandchildren,
and the flocks and herds all going?

130

God did keep his promise to Abraham!
He did make him into a great nation.
When God's people left Egypt,
there were almost one million of them!

Do you know what God did next?

God gave this great nation his good word.

Moses went up on a mountaintop to meet with God.
The mountain shook, and lightning flashed.
God spoke to Moses, and then
Moses told the people all that God had said.

133

Moses told them how to love God.
Moses told them how to love others.
Moses told them how to live as God's people.

And to make sure that no one would forget,
Moses had God's words written down
in God's holy book.
But do you know what happened?
Something sad.

134

135

God's people still forgot God's Word.

Many of them doubted that God's Word was good.
Many of them disobeyed God's Word.
Many of them did not let God be king over them.

137

So God punished his people.
He made them live in the desert for a long, long time.

But after forty years,
God was ready to keep another part of his promise.

God was ready to bring his people into their own place.

GOING INTO GOD'S PLACE

Part 8

God's special place was called Canaan.
And God chose a man named Joshua
to lead his people into it.

But there was a problem.

Other people already lived in Canaan.

143

They lived in cities like Jericho
with big, strong walls around them.
The cities were filled with
people who did not listen to God.

God told Joshua,
"Be strong and courageous."

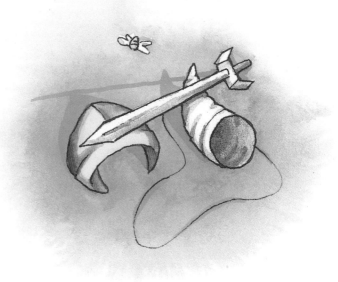

God told Joshua to have the people
march around Jericho six days in a row.

So the people marched and marched all day long—
one, two, three, four, five, six whole days they marched.

Do you know what happened on the seventh day?
When the trumpets sounded and the people shouted . . .

God kept his promise, and
the walls came tumbling down!

God drove out their enemies.

Then God's people lived in the land he had promised them.

149

150

When Joshua was an old man,
he reminded the people to obey God's Word.
"Choose this day whom you will serve. . . .
But as for me and my house,
we will serve the Lord."

And the people said,
"We also will serve the Lord."

152

On that day,
many of God's good promises
to Israel were fulfilled.

153

Israel promised to be God's people.
Israel promised to obey God's Word.
If they kept their promises,
they would always live in God's promised place.

But after Joshua died . . .

Israel disobeyed God's Word and rejected God from being king over them.

156

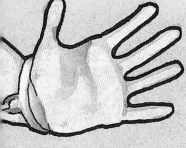

So God punished Israel.

He let their enemies rule over them.

During this time the Philistines ruled God's people.
One of the Philistines was so big and strong
that not one of God's people would fight him.
Goliath was a giant.
He stood over nine feet tall.

Goliath hated God's people.

All the men of Israel were afraid of him.

All except one.

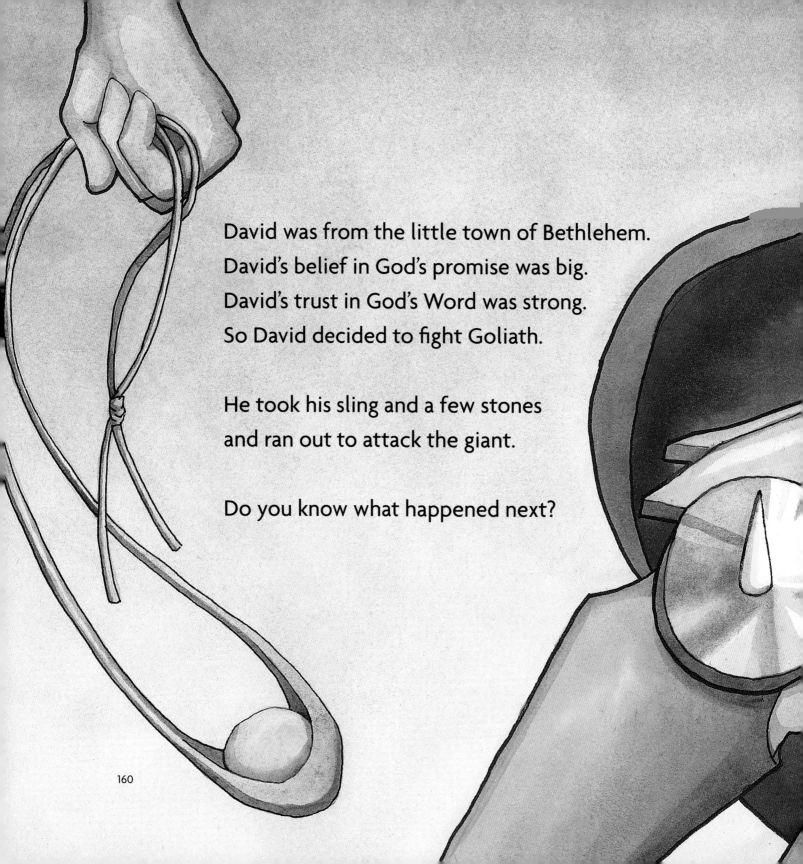

David was from the little town of Bethlehem.
David's belief in God's promise was big.
David's trust in God's Word was strong.
So David decided to fight Goliath.

He took his sling and a few stones
and ran out to attack the giant.

Do you know what happened next?

161

God kept his promise
to rescue his people!

The first stone that flew from
David's sling hit Goliath
right between the eyes.

162

David killed Goliath and rescued
Israel from the Philistines.

163

God was with David.
And God gave David victory
over his enemies in other battles.

David, the mighty warrior,
became king over God's people.
David ruled over God's special place.

Do you see David singing to God?
He is thanking God for keeping his promises.

Now that God's people were in God's place,
it seemed that soon they would become a blessing
to all the peoples of the earth.

GOD'S BLESSINGS GROW

Part 9

David was amazed at how good God was.
David wanted to do something nice for God.
David decided to build God a house.

But one night God sent word to David.
He didn't want David to build him a house.
God said that David's son would build the house instead.

170

Then God surprised David.
God promised to build David a house!
Not a real house made of bricks or wood
but a kingdom—God's kingdom.

And then God surprised David again!
God promised him that someone from David's
family would live forever as God's king.

If that weren't enough, God surprised David again!
This forever ruler would be the promised one
who would bring God's blessing to all the
peoples of the earth.

God's surprising promise
made David very happy!
He thanked God, and the
promise was written in
God's holy book.

After David died . . .

173

David's son Solomon became king.

With gold and wood he built God a great house.
It was a beautiful place called a temple.

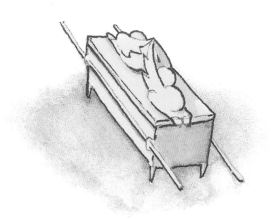

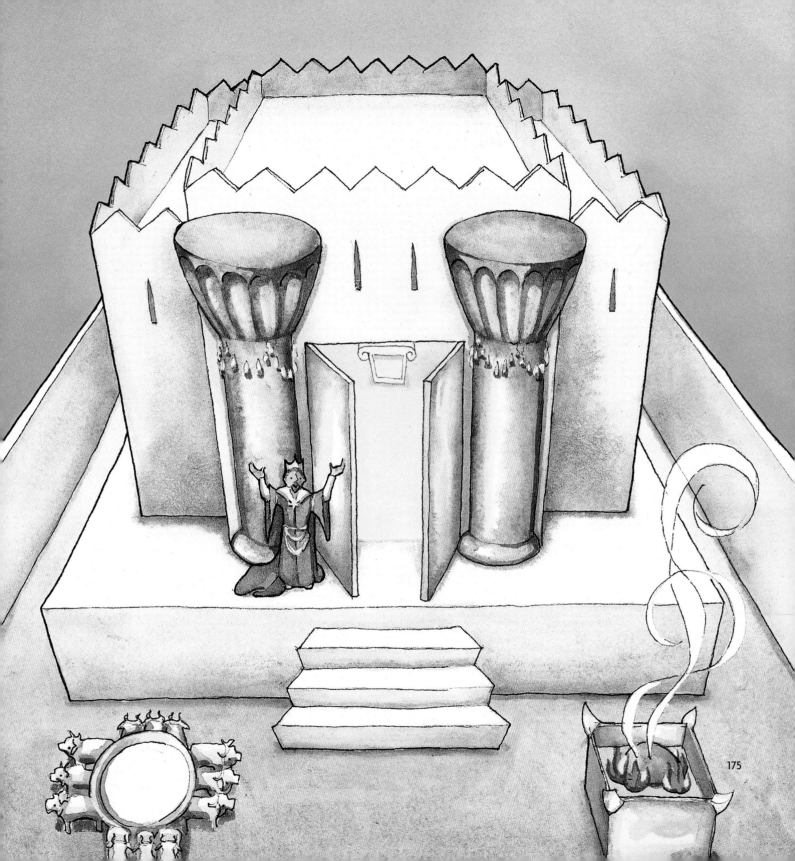

This temple was
where the people
made blood
sacrifices for
their sins.
When God saw
that great sign,
he would forgive,
or pass over,
the sins of his
people.

After the temple was finished,
God came down in a cloud.
The people were happy and gave
thanks to the Lord saying,
"He is good, for his steadfast
love endures forever."

A queen came to see Solomon,
his palace, and the temple he had built.

She asked him lots of questions,
and God gave Solomon wisdom for them all.
The queen was amazed and greatly helped by all he said
and was *blessed* by God for having come.

You see, God was keeping
all his promises to Abraham.

He had already made Abraham into a great nation.
And he had given Israel the land.
And now God's king was bringing God's blessing
to other peoples of the earth.

Does this make you wonder
if Solomon might be God's forever king?
Could he be the promised one to bring
God's blessings to everyone?

Part 10

King Solomon turned his heart away from God.
God's people turned their
hearts away from God too.

188

They doubted that God was good.
They disobeyed God's Word.
They rejected God as their king.

189

Before Solomon died, God told him that someday
his kingdom would be torn apart.
After Solomon died, God's Word came true.

God was angry. He sent prophets
to warn God's kings and people
to stop disobeying God's Word.

One of those prophets was Elijah.

191

At that time the ruler over part of God's people was Ahab.
Elijah challenged Ahab's prophets to a contest.

He told the prophets to ask their god to send down fire on an altar.
King Ahab's prophets asked and asked and asked, but fire never came.

Then Elijah built an altar.
He told the people to pour four big jars of water on his altar.
Then he told them to do it again, and again!
Twelve jars of water soaked Elijah's altar.

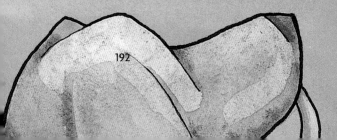

Only then did Elijah step forward and pray,

"O Lord, God of Abraham, Isaac, and Israel,

let it be known this day that you are God in Israel....

Answer me ... that this people may know that you,

O Lord, are God, and that you have turned their hearts back."

And do you know what happened then?

God answered Elijah's prayer!

196

Fire fell from the sky and burned
up Elijah's sacrifice.
God's fire burned up the stones, the soil,
and all the water that had soaked the altar.

The people were amazed!

But do you think this made them return to God?
No, it didn't.
They continued to
disobey God's Word.

So . . .

198

199

God punished his people
by sending a ruler from far
away to make war on them.
Many of God's people were
killed or taken away.

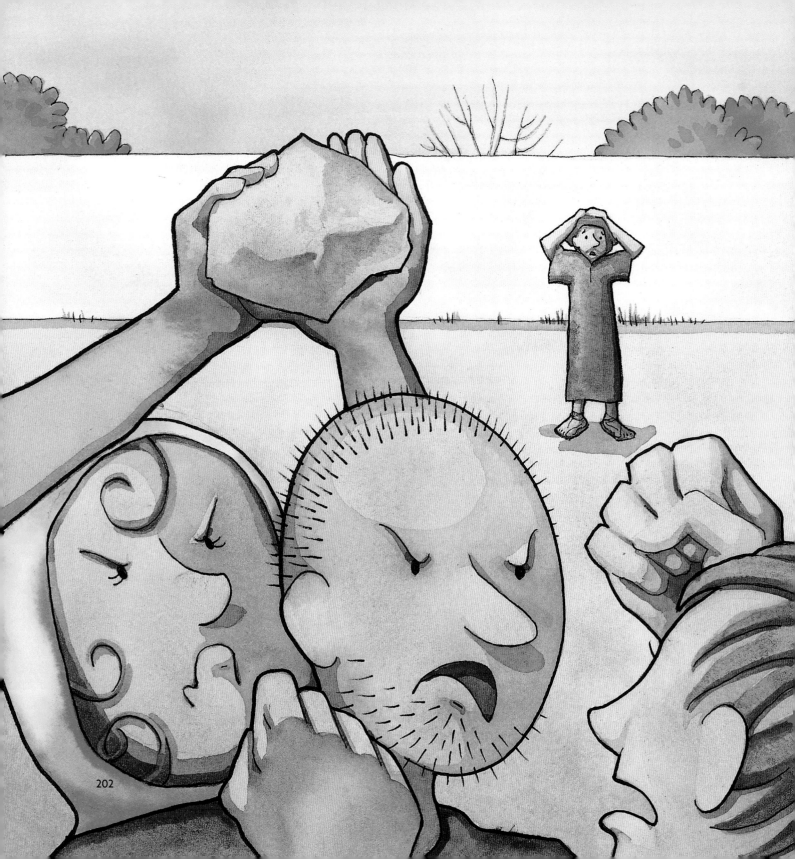

Later King Zedekiah ruled over the rest of God's people.
He did many evil things, and still
he did not think that God would punish him.

He thought to himself,

Didn't God promise us this land forever?

So God sent the prophet Jeremiah to say to the king, "No."

But Zedekiah refused to listen.

So . . .

God punished his people again
by sending another king to make war on them.

King Nebuchadnezzar came all the way
from Babylon, and he destroyed Jerusalem.
He burned Solomon's temple to the ground
and took the rest of God's people
far away from their land.

This was another very sad day.

God's people had to leave God's place because they would not have God for their king.

Do you remember when God sent Adam and Eve away from him out of the garden?

Well, God was doing it again.
He was sending his people out of his place
because of their sin.

GOD'S PROMISE REMAINS

Part 11

Even though God's people were far from home,
God still spoke to them.

God sent more prophets.
They spoke all his words and
wrote them down in God's holy book.

The prophet Ezekiel wrote that one day God would raise up the temple and give his people new hearts.

Isaiah reminded them that God's forever king would come from the family of David.

The prophet Jeremiah was hopeful too. He said that Israel would return home again in seventy years.

Seventy years passed, and the prophet
Daniel prayed to God.
He asked God to remember his
promise, and God heard Daniel's prayer.

Finally God's people went home
to Jerusalem.
They returned to the land.
But they had a lot of work to do.
Jerusalem and the temple were ruined.

They worked very hard.
And when the foundation
was finished ...

Can you see the
people rebuilding the city
walls and the temple?

221

The people celebrated!

All the people shouted loud praises to God.
They were happy.
With trumpets and cymbals they sang to God:

"For he is good, for his steadfast love
endures forever...."

223

But many of the older men cried.
Can you guess why?

They cried because they remembered
Solomon's beautiful temple and knew that
Israel could never completely rebuild God's place.

225

226

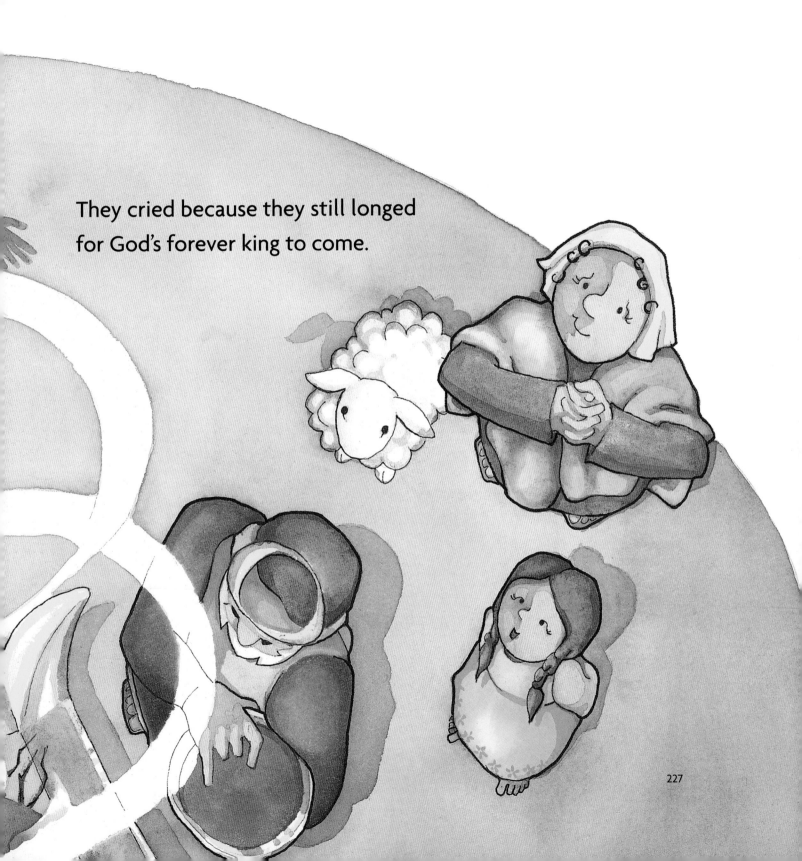

They cried because they still longed for God's forever king to come.

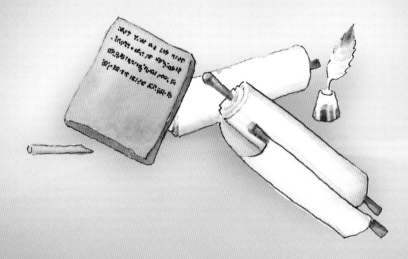

THE NEW TESTAMENT

MANY SILENT YEARS

Part 12

Years passed

without a single word from God.

And the years turned into many years,
and the many years turned into hundreds of years,
and the great promises of God seemed to fade away.

Israel became less important in the world.
Other nations became great—
strong nations,
powerful nations
whose kings ruled over God's people.

One such king . . .

Was Caesar Augustus.

This Roman ruler thought he was very important.
One day he wondered to himself,
How will everyone know that I am
the great Caesar,
the Roman ruler,
the king of the world?

I know!
I will count all the people under my rule.
Surely that will show the world how great I am.

So Caesar, the Roman ruler,
the king of the whole Roman world,
began counting all his people to show
everyone how great he was.

What Caesar did not know was that . . .

238

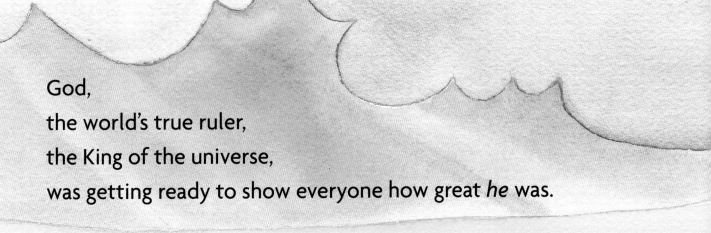

God,
the world's true ruler,
the King of the universe,
was getting ready to show everyone how great *he* was.

God was going to end his many years of silence.
God was going to keep his promise of a forever king.

And do you know how God was going to do this?
Not like Caesar . . .
not proudly, by counting all his people,
but humbly, by becoming one of his people.

In the power of his Spirit, God would bring his forever king into the world as a baby!

GOD'S PROMISED ONE IS BORN

Part 13

Look at all the people on the road to Bethlehem.

They were on their way to be counted,
and they were very unhappy.

They were mad at the king,
and they frowned as they walked.
They were angry with the king,
and they grumbled as they walked.

But not everyone was unhappy.
Do you see the happy couple on the road?

If they were mad at the king, their faces didn't show it.
Do you have any idea why they were so happy?

248

Mary soon was going to have a baby!

God had told Mary and Joseph that
their baby was the one promised long ago.
He would rescue God's people,
give God's place back to them,
and bless all the peoples of the earth.

But in this crowded city,
where would this
special baby be born?

In a nice, big home?
No, not in a nice, big home.

In a clean hotel?
No, not in a clean hotel.

All the nice, big homes
and clean hotels
were filled up with people.

Can you guess where this
special baby would be born?

God's forever King was born
in a stable, a place for animals.

His parents named him Jesus.
They wrapped him up warmly
and laid him in a manger.

What a strange place for the Promised One!
Who would have imagined it?

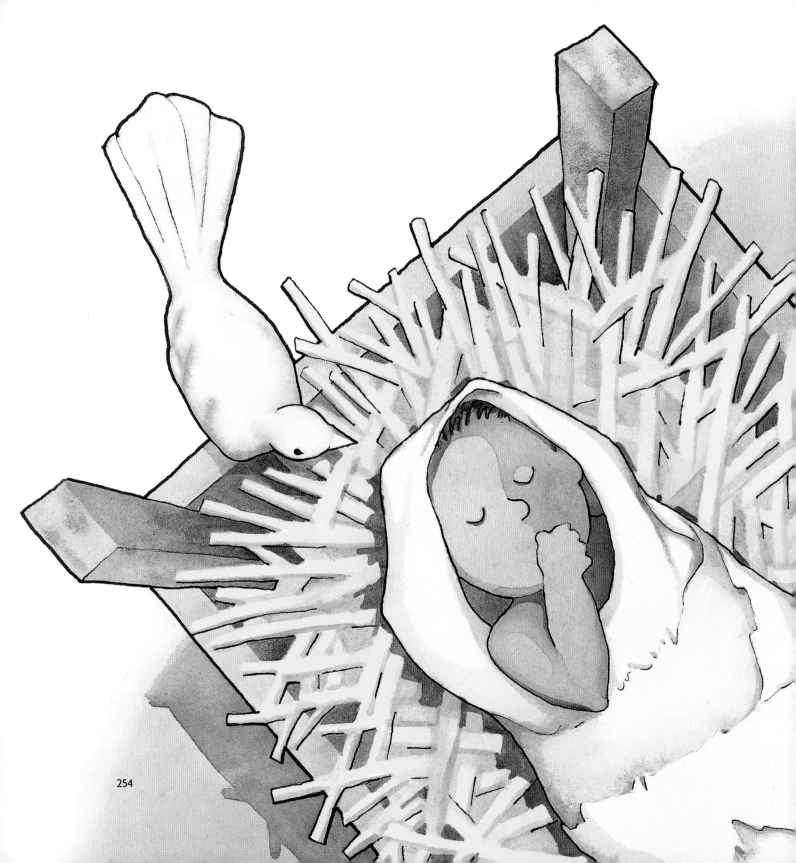

While Caesar, the King of the Roman world,
was showing everyone how great he was
by counting all of his people,

God, the King of the universe,
was showing the world how great *he* was
by sending his Son into the world as one of his people.

What a very big day!

What God had promised to Abraham, Isaac, Jacob, and David had arrived in the birth of Jesus!

And news of his great arrival was about to spread.

257

GOD'S PROMISED ONE IS ANNOUNCED

Part 14

Look at all those sheep.
Do you see the men watching over the sheep?
They are shepherds.

On the night that Jesus was born,
out on the rolling hills of Bethlehem,
some shepherds were enjoying the cool air.

It was dark.
It was quiet.
And then all of a sudden . . .
God surprised the shepherds!

A bright light shone in the night sky.
An angel made a big announcement
to the shepherds:

"I bring you good news . . . for all the people.
For unto you is born this day in the city of David
a Savior, who is Christ the Lord. . . .
You will find a baby wrapped in swaddling cloths
 and lying in a manger."

The shepherds were so amazed!
And then there was another surprise.

More and more and more angels came,
until the night sky was filled with
wonder and brightness.

Together they sang,
"Glory to God in the highest, and on earth peace
among those with whom he is pleased!"

At this, the shepherds ran to
Bethlehem as fast as they could.
They wanted to see
the long-awaited promise
of God lying in a manger.

266

And when they got there,
they saw the baby Jesus.

267

They smiled. They knew.
Everything the angels had
told them was true!

Jesus, God's forever King,
had been born!

GOD'S NEW PEOPLE ARE CALLED

Part 15

Thirty years passed,
and Jesus grew from a baby into a man.

Thirty years passed,
and the world still had not heard
the message the angels had sung to the shepherds.

Thirty years passed,
and so far no one had become a follower of Jesus.
Do you know how God told people
they should follow his Son?

273

God didn't use angels this time.
Instead, God used a man.

This man was already teaching
people about God's kingdom.
This man lived in the desert,
and his name was . . .

John.

John did not dress like most of God's people.
John did not eat like most of God's people.
John did not speak like most of God's people.

But that did not keep God's people
from coming out to the desert to listen to John.

John was baptizing people
to get them ready for the coming kingdom of God.

People came from the hills and valleys.
They came from big cities and small towns.

In fact, so many people came that
some began to wonder,
"Could John be the prophet sent to rescue us?
Could John be the one to give us back God's place?
Could John be the king who will bless all the people
of the earth?"

John told them,

"No. I am not the Promised One,
but I am preparing the way for the King."

And then one day when John was
baptizing people in the river . . .

Jesus came to him and
asked to be baptized.

When John baptized Jesus,
a dove flew down and rested on Jesus.
A loud voice came from heaven:
"You are my beloved Son;
with you I am well pleased."

John told the people that Jesus was
God's promised King.

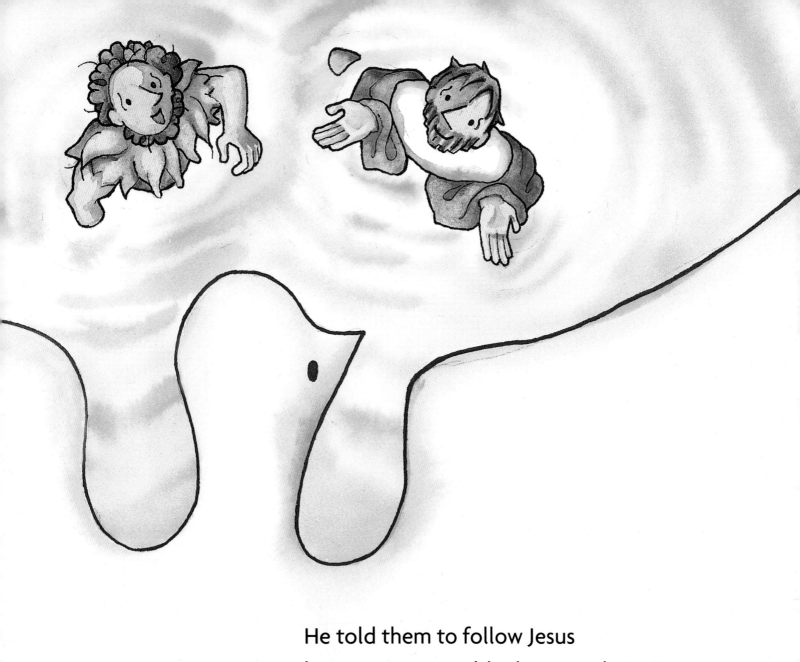

He told them to follow Jesus
because Jesus could take away their sin.

People began to listen to Jesus preach about the
kingdom of God.
And to some he said, "Follow me."

Jesus chose twelve followers to be his special disciples.
Do you remember Jacob's twelve sons?
Well, Jesus was beginning to call out
a new people for God.

JESUS RESTORES GOD'S PLACE

Part 16

287

One day Jesus was walking through the temple.
This was the place where people went to meet with God.

This temple wasn't the one that Solomon had built.
And it wasn't the one that Israel had rebuilt either.
No, those temples had been destroyed hundreds
of years before.

Herod had built this temple.
The Romans had made Herod king.
Herod was clever and tricky.

He built this place to keep God's people happy so
they would obey him as king.

While walking through the temple . . .

Jesus saw men selling cattle
and sheep and doves.

Jesus saw other greedy men sitting at tables trading money.

Seeing all this made Jesus angry.
The temple was supposed to be a holy place.
This was the place where blood sacrifices for sin were made.

Instead, the temple had become a wicked place.

People came to look important

and to put lots of money in their own pockets.

People were sinning instead of coming to be forgiven.

What Jesus saw made him so angry that . . .

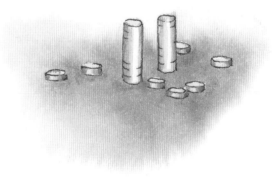

He did something about it.

He tipped over the tables of the money traders,
and all the coins scattered.
He made a whip and drove out the sheep and the cattle,
and all the doves scattered.

And while he was doing this . . .

Jesus demanded:
"Take these things away;
do not make my Father's house
a house of trade."

296

That made the people angry,
and they yelled back, as if to say,
"Hey, who do you think you are?
Prove to us that you are
in charge of this place!"

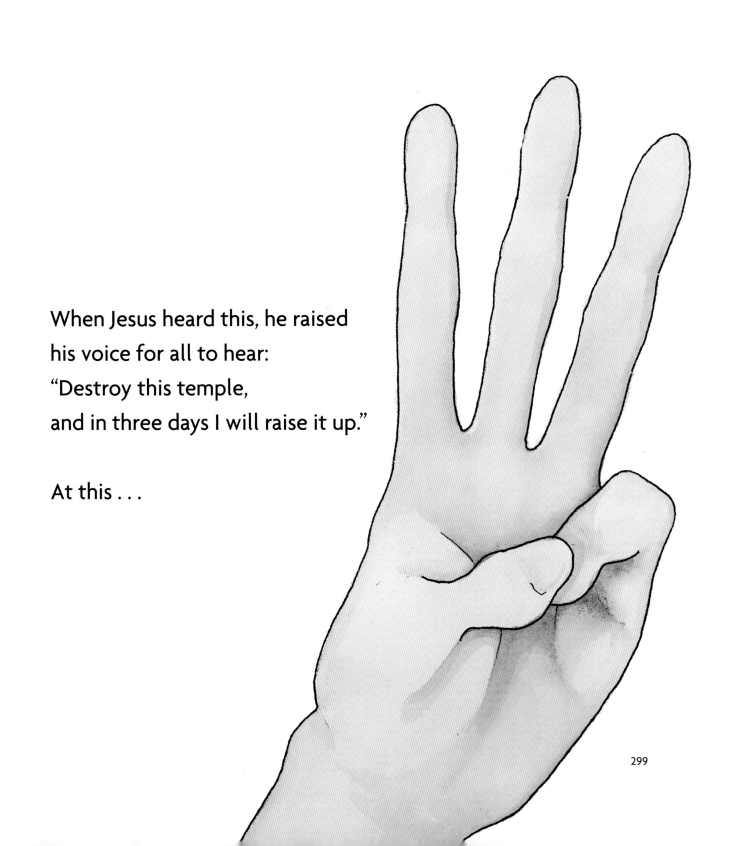

When Jesus heard this, he raised
his voice for all to hear:
"Destroy this temple,
and in three days I will raise it up."

At this . . .

Everyone got quiet.

300

The leaders of God's place
scratched their heads;
they closed their eyes,
and they thought,
Surely, this man is confused.

Finally one of them said to Jesus,
"It has taken forty-six years to build this temple,
and will you raise it up in three days?"

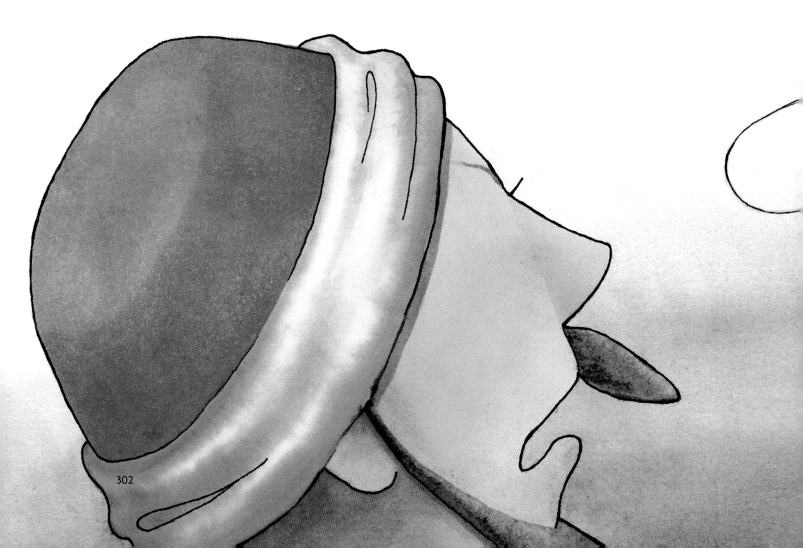

Jesus didn't answer.
Jesus just walked away.
He was right. The leaders did not understand
what he was saying about God's special place.

303

This stone temple wasn't God's place anymore.

Jesus was God's special place.
His body was God's holy temple.
His blood would pay for sins.

He was better than the places
built by Solomon, the Israelites, or Herod.

But on that day no one understood Jesus,
although there was a man who thought he did.

JESUS REVEALS GOD'S KINGDOM

Part 17

One night, long after most people were asleep,
a man walked along the streets of Jerusalem.

The man's name was Nicodemus.

Do you see him?

He was one of the leaders who liked Jesus.

But he also thought that Jesus was mistaken.

309

He knew what Jesus
had done in the
temple.
And he wanted
to remind Jesus that
the temple was
an important place in
God's kingdom.

310

At last he found the home where Jesus was staying.

311

Jesus and Nicodemus
sat down to talk.

312

Nicodemus began,
"We know that you are a
teacher come from God,
for no one can do these
signs that you do unless
God is with him."

Jesus replied,
"Unless one is born again
he cannot see the
kingdom of God."

314

Nicodemus was surprised.
"How can a man be born when he is old?
Can he enter a second time
into his mother's womb and be born?"

Then Jesus told Nicodemus that no one can enter
the kingdom of God unless he is born again.

Nicodemus did not understand.

Couldn't he see the kingdom of God
without being born again?
After all, he could see the temple.
Wasn't that a sign of God's kingdom?

Couldn't he enter the kingdom
without being born again?
After all, he was in Abraham's family line.
Wasn't that a sign that he had already entered
the kingdom of God when he was born?

317

Jesus hinted from God's holy book
about God's Spirit who brings new life.
He tried to help Nicodemus understand.

Jesus explained
that Nicodemus had not been
born into God's kingdom.
Instead, God's kingdom had to be born in him.

But, sad to say, Nicodemus, a teacher of
God's holy book, did not yet understand.

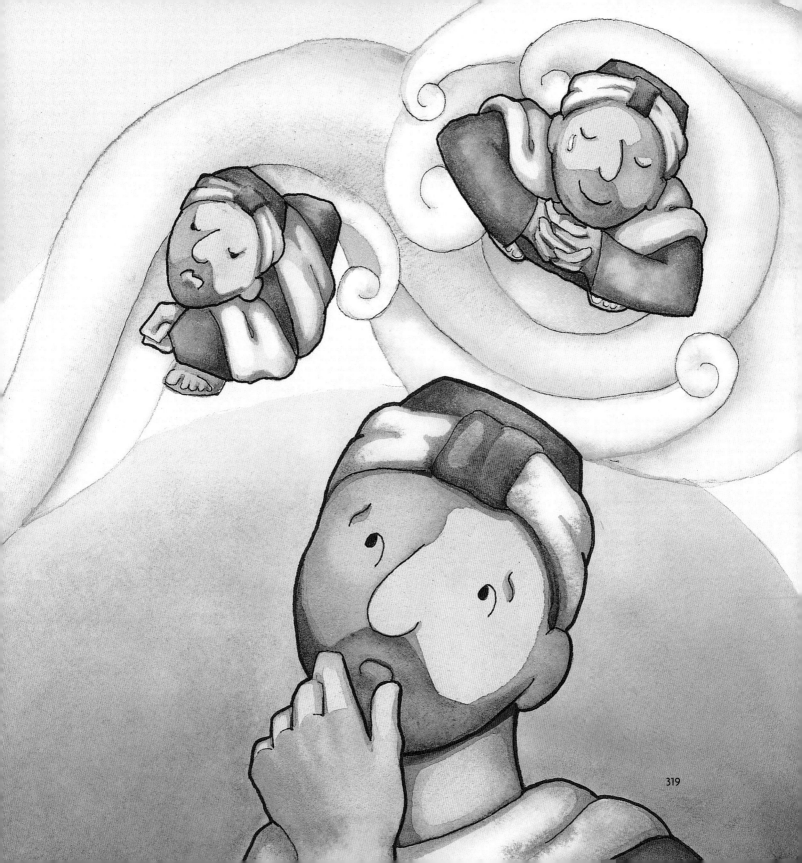

He went out again into the dark night confused.
But some would understand.
Others would not take so long to believe
that Jesus was sent from God.
Others would see and be born again.

Part 18

One day as Jesus walked along,
he saw a man blind from birth—
a man who could not see.

Jesus's disciples asked him who had disobeyed God, " . . . this man or his parents, that he was born blind?"

Jesus said there was a different reason why this man was born blind. Jesus told them to watch and see the work God had sent him to do.

So the disciples watched as . . .

326

Jesus walked over to the blind man and spat
upon the ground.
He made some mud with the spit and put it
on the blind man's eyes.
Then Jesus said,
"Go, wash in the pool of Siloam"
(which means Sent).

So the man went.
And the man washed.

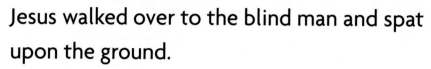

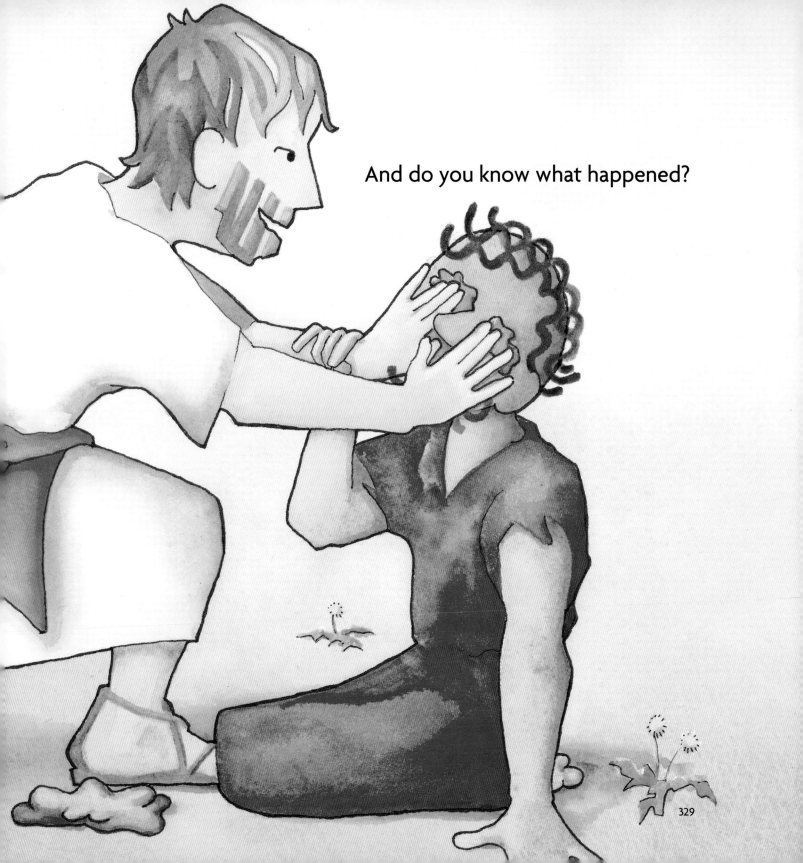

And do you know what happened?

329

When the man opened his eyes
again, he could see!
By this miracle God showed
everyone that Jesus had been
sent to do God's work.

330

331

Now some of the leaders
listened to the man's story,
but they did not believe that Jesus had
made him see.
They said of Jesus,
"This man is not from God."

But the man who had been blind knew better.
He told them that Jesus must have come from God.
This made the leaders so angry that . . .

They threw the man
out of the temple.
Later Jesus found the man.
Jesus told him that God had sent
him into the world
to make people see that he could
rescue them from sin.

The man now saw who Jesus
really was, and he believed.

A DEAD MAN IS RAISED TO LIFE

Part 19

A man named Lazarus was very sick.
His sisters, Mary and Martha,
knew that he was dying.
They wanted Jesus to come
and heal Lazarus.
So they sent for Jesus.

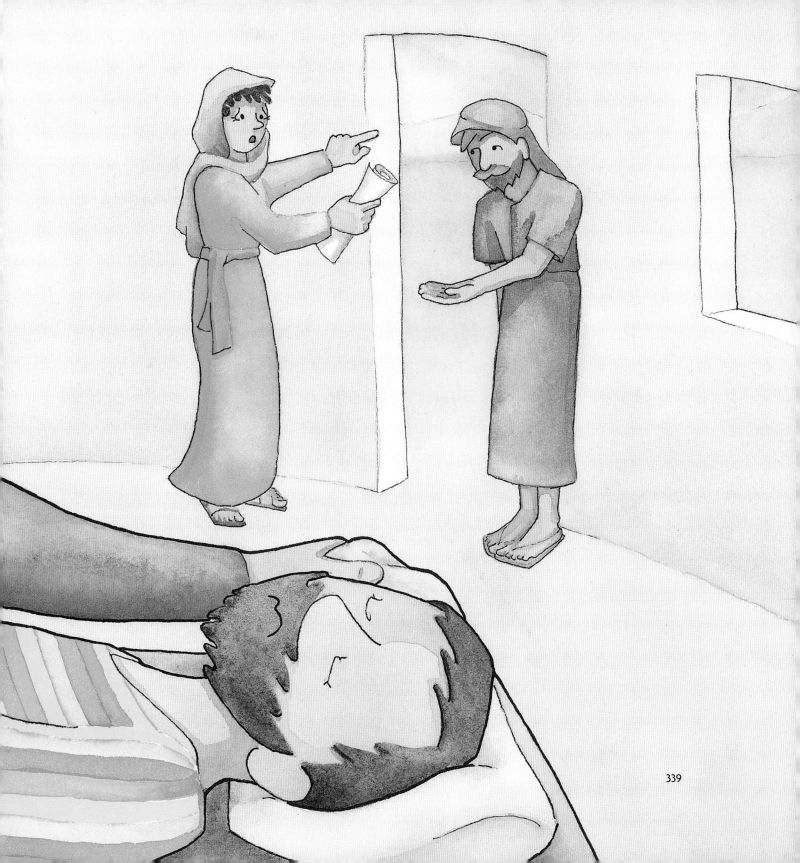

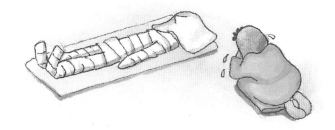

Jesus loved his friends, but when he heard
Lazarus was sick, he did a surprising thing.
He stayed where he was.
He did not come right away.

Jesus knew God was going to use him
to do something amazing.
Jesus was going to show
God's power over death.

So Jesus waited until Lazarus died,
and then he went to be with his friends.

By the time Jesus got there, Lazarus had been in a tomb for four days.

Martha met him and said,
"Lord, if you had been here,
my brother would
not have died."

Jesus replied,
"Your brother will rise again. . . .
I am the resurrection and the life.
Whoever believes in me, though he
die, yet shall he live. . . .
Do you believe this?"

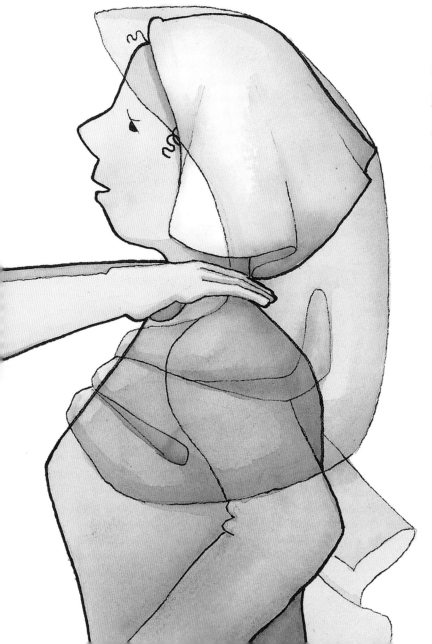

Martha said yes.
She believed that Jesus
was God's King and Son
who was sent to
bring life to the world.

Then Mary came to see Jesus,
and Jesus saw her crying.
He went with Mary to the tomb.
And then Jesus cried too.

Some who were there saw Jesus and said,
"Could not he who opened the eyes of the blind man
also have kept this man from dying?"

347

They did not know that Jesus
was getting ready to show them that God
had sent him to rescue people from sin and death.

Jesus told them to open the tomb.
Only then did Jesus step forward and pray,
"Father, I thank you that you have heard me. . . .
I said this . . . that they may believe
that you sent me."

Then in a really loud voice, Jesus shouted, "Lazarus, come out!"

And do you know what happened?

351

God answered Jesus's prayer!

Lazarus came out. He was alive.
A dead man was now alive again.

Jesus showed the people that God's
Spirit had power to bring new life.

Many people believed in Jesus on that day.

They believed:
Here is the one who will rescue God's people.
Here is the one who has become God's place.
Here is the one who even rules over death
and can bring God's blessing to all the peoples
of the earth.

The people were ready
to make Jesus their King!

355

But that made the leaders angry.
They were jealous of Jesus.

They hated him and did
not want him as their King.

They decided that the time had come.
They would kill him as soon as they could.

Part 20

Jesus knew his time had come. Soon he would be King!

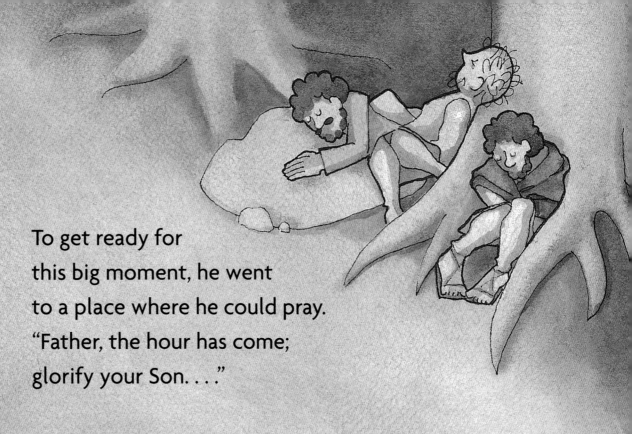

To get ready for
this big moment, he went
to a place where he could pray.
"Father, the hour has come;
glorify your Son. . . ."

Jesus worked hard praying.
But the disciples were tired, and they
slept as Jesus prayed.

When Jesus finished, he woke them up.

He told them that his time had come.
Just then . . .

Some people who hated Jesus marched up to them.
They brought soldiers with them too.

362

These men didn't believe Jesus
was God's forever King.
They tied up his hands
and arrested him.
Jesus's followers ran away.

The soldiers and some leaders took Jesus
to a place where they hit him in the face.

Then they led him off to Pilate,
a Roman ruler, and said,
"Jesus is trying to take over as king!
A criminal like this should die.
He should not be king.
We would rather be ruled by Rome
than by this pretend king."

"Crucify him, Pilate."

365

Pilate talked to Jesus.
He asked him,
"Are you the King?"

Jesus answered,
"My kingdom is
not of this world."

Pilate did not think Jesus was trouble.
Pilate did not think Jesus was a threat
to Roman rule.
Pilate may have thought to himself,

If I can show the people
that I am in control,
then they will let him go.

So . . .

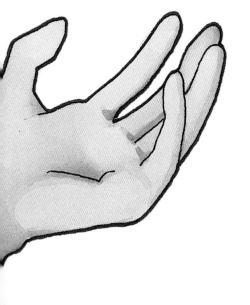

Pilate had Jesus beaten.
The soldiers whipped
him many times.

They laughed at the
idea of Jesus as King.
They dressed him in
a purple robe.

They made a crown
of thorns and put it
on his head.

They punched him and
made fun of him:
"Hail, King of the Jews!"

Then Pilate tried to let Jesus go.

But the people only shouted louder.
They wanted to kill Jesus.
They warned Pilate that the time had come.

So Pilate decided to have Jesus killed.
He looked out only for himself.

And so . . .

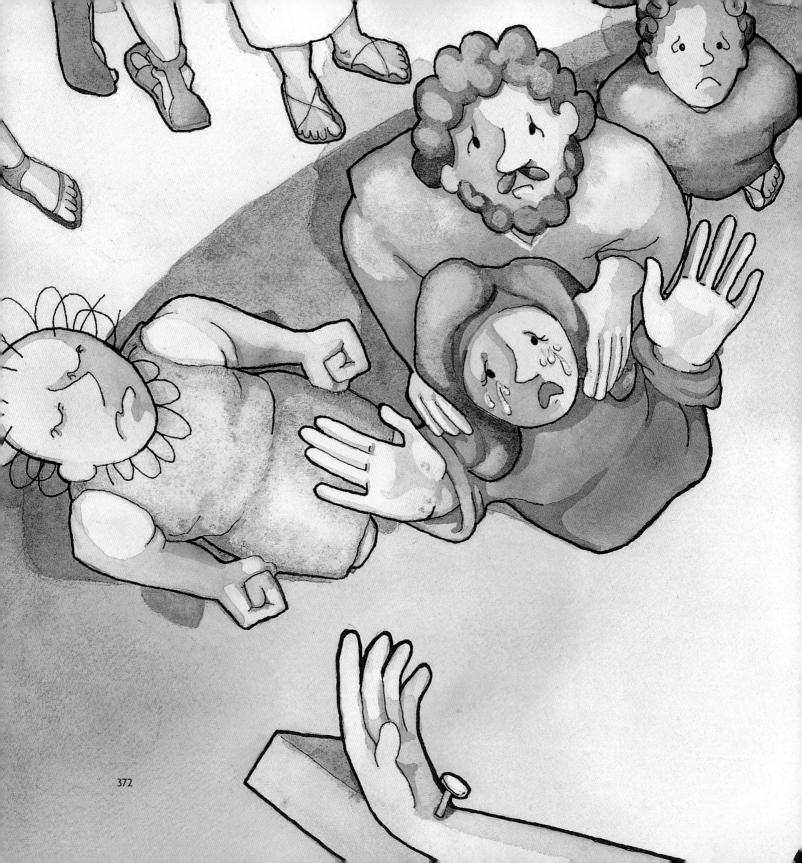

On a small hill
outside the city
of Jerusalem,
Jesus
was nailed to a cross,
and died.

JESUS'S FOLLOWERS ARE IN THE DARK

Part 21

Darkness fell upon the land.

Jesus was dead.
He was buried in a tomb.
A big stone was rolled in front
of the entrance,
and the people all went home.
For Jesus's followers, that dark day
was followed by a long night.

The hours passed very slowly.
Jesus's friends cried.
They had thought he was the King.

But now their hearts were filled with sorrow,
and their minds were filled with fear.

"What happened?"
"Why did Jesus have to die?"
"Wasn't Jesus God's forever King?"

The questions kept coming until the next
day turned into night.

As Jesus's followers tried to sleep, they thought,
We will be sad forever.

"Will God ever rescue his *people* from sin?"

"Will we ever have our *place* with him?"

"Will God ever bring again his blessings on *all peoples of the earth?*"

A BRAND-NEW DAY

Part 22

It was the third day after Jesus
had died on the cross.
The sun was not yet up.

One woman, Mary Magdalene,
couldn't sleep.
She had believed in Jesus and
had hoped he was the King.

She got up very early
while it was still dark
and went to the tomb where
Jesus was buried.

As she came close,
suddenly she grew
anxious and afraid.
The big stone that covered
the entrance was gone.
Jesus's tomb was open,
and it was empty.

She turned and ran.
She did not stop.

Seeing two of Jesus's followers,
she caught her breath and cried,
"They have taken the Lord out of the tomb."

Her friends ran off!
They raced to
the tomb.
They looked around;
they went inside,
but Jesus was
not there.

390

As they walked
back home,
they wondered
what had happened.

That evening . . .

Some of Jesus's followers were meeting together.
They were afraid, and so
they had locked the doors.

Suddenly Jesus came and stood among them!
At first his followers were frightened,
but then their fear turned into joy.

393

The sadness they had felt was gone.
Their hearts were glad again.

Jesus was alive.
Jesus really was alive.
Jesus was risen from the dead.

The Son had risen!
It was a brand-new day.

GOD'S PROMISE IS EXPLAINED

Part 23

Jesus's followers could hardly believe it.
"We have seen the Lord!"

They were full of joy,
but they were not full
of understanding.

398

They could see Jesus
with their eyes,
but they could not
see why he had
to die and
rise again.

And so . . .

Jesus opened up God's holy book
that had been written long ago.
He started with the books of Moses
and then the Prophets and the Psalms.
He showed them everything
that was written there about him.

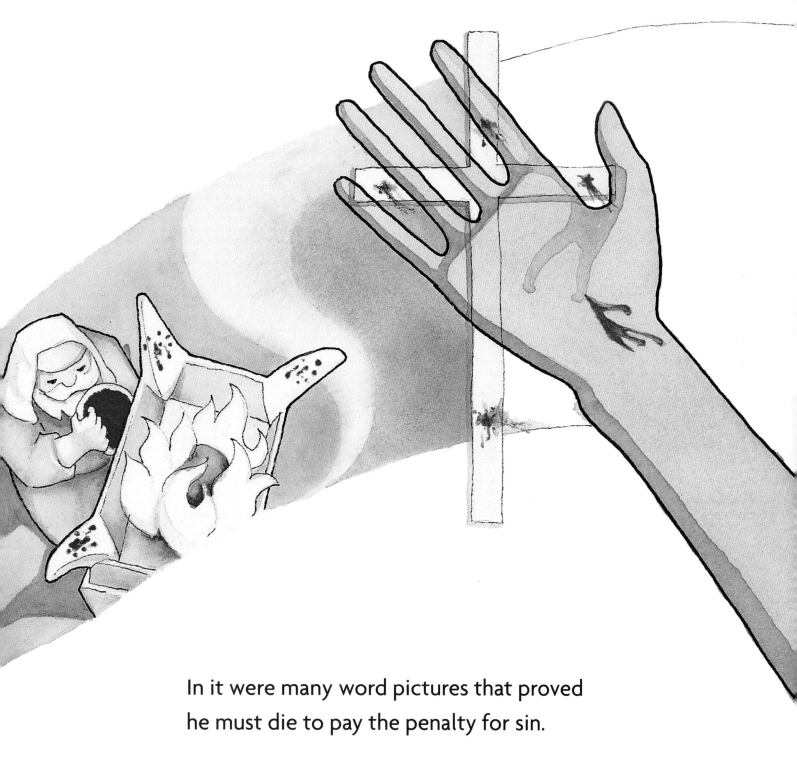

In it were many word pictures that proved
he must die to pay the penalty for sin.

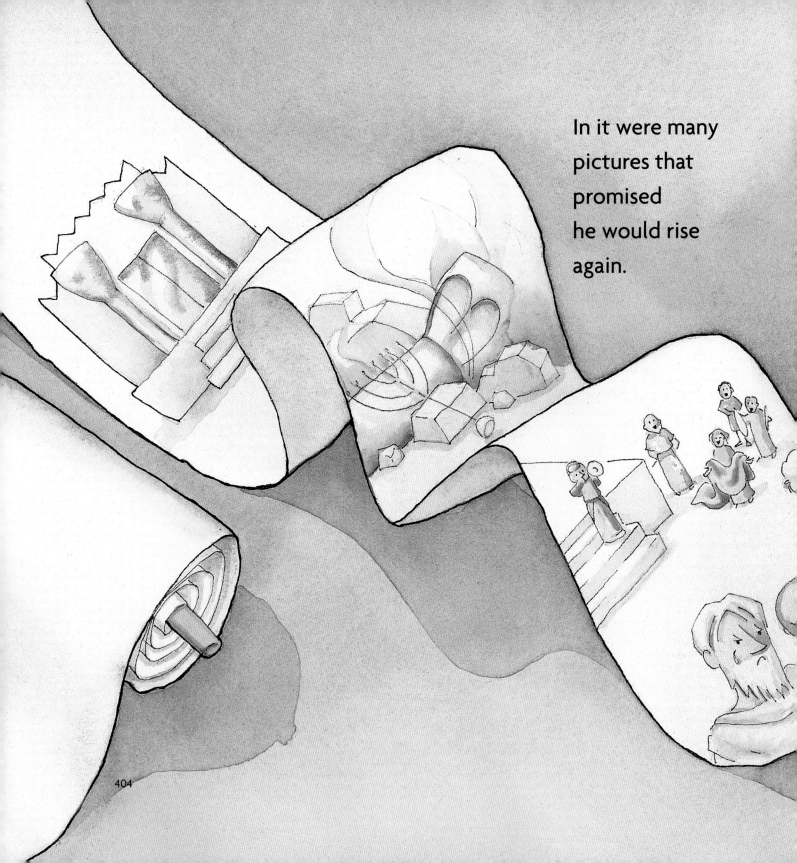

In it were many pictures that promised he would rise again.

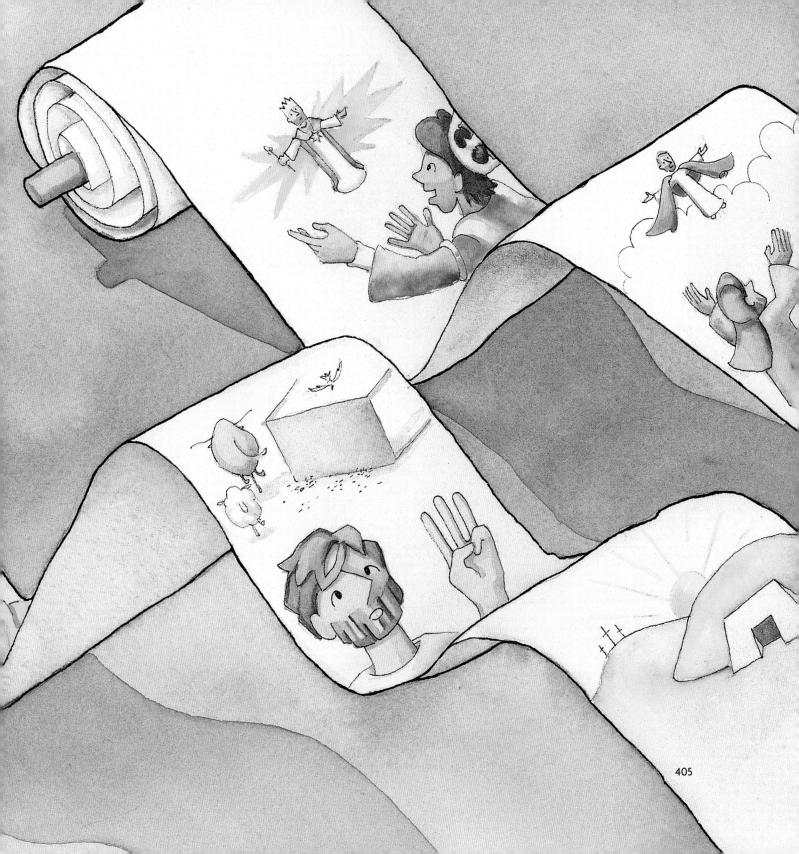

Jesus's followers were amazed
as they listened and as they read.

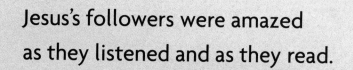

Before, they had said,
"We have seen the Lord!"

But now they could read God's
holy book and say,

"Even here, especially here,
we have seen the Lord!"

407

Jesus taught them carefully because
he knew the day was coming
when people would no longer
see him with their eyes.
They would read of him instead.

He knew God's holy book would
help others to believe and say,
"We have seen the Lord!"
And they too would be full of joy.

Do you see the Lord?

Painted on the pages of Israel's
hard and happy history is the
big picture of God's forever King.

GOD'S NEW KINGDOM SPREADS

Part 24

For forty days after his resurrection
Jesus taught about God's kingdom.

He told his chosen followers
that they had kingdom
work to do.
He said that although
he must go away for a time,
they must wait for a gift
he would send to help
them do that work.

416

And then suddenly Jesus left them.
He was lifted up into the sky.
He took his throne in heaven
and began his kingly rule.

His followers went back to Jerusalem and waited.
They waited and waited for the promised gift.

Ten days passed, and . . .

Then they heard something.
There was a loud sound like
the wind blowing.
It came from heaven and
filled the room.

Then they saw something.
Little flames of fire
floated overhead
and came to rest on each
of them.

Then they said something. They were praising God in languages that they had never learned.

The promised gift, the Holy Spirit, had come to them!

Other people also heard the wind and the voices.
But they didn't recognize the Holy Spirit.
They wondered if Jesus's followers were drunk.

Peter raised his voice
and spoke:
"These men are not
drunk, as you suppose. . . ."

He told them of the prophets who had
said God would send his Spirit.
He told them of Jesus's death and how
God had raised him to life again.
He told them to repent and to believe
in God's forever King.

This news entered into their hearts.
Many confessed their sins
and believed.
On that special day, God's Spirit
gave new life to many.
God's people were growing in number again!

And as the good news of God's
kingdom spread, still more people
repented and believed.

The good news spread
and spread and spread!

The word that was preached
in Jerusalem went out all
across the land.

It spread to
people in Judea.

It spread to Samaria too.

Later the apostle Paul
spread it as far away
as Rome.

425

Far and near, people from every nation
were beginning to follow Jesus as their King.

LETTERS TO LIVE BY

Part 25

Look at all these people!

Women and men,
girls and boys,
young and old
from many
different nations,
decided to follow
Jesus as their King.

They had not seen Jesus face to face.
They had not talked with him or heard him teach.
And those who had been with Jesus
could not be with them all the time.

Would God's people know what to do?

God knew what to do for his people!

God chose some of Jesus's special followers
to write letters to complete God's holy book.

These letters told God's people:
"Remember, hold on to the message.
Keep believing in Jesus!
Love one another like family. Forgive one another.
Be careful! Don't let people trick you.
Run away from sin. Endure hardship.
And look for Jesus's return."

Everywhere that God's kingdom spread
these letters could be found.
They helped God's people grow in faith.
They made God's young church strong.

THE VERY GOOD ENDING

Part 26

Do you see the man writing?

His name is John.
Long ago he had run with Peter
to the empty tomb.
Later he had traveled far and wide,
telling others of God's King.
But now John was very old.

He would not be doing much
traveling or speaking anymore.
People who didn't believe his
message had seen to that!
They were keeping John here
as a prisoner.

But God had a big surprise for John.
There was one more place for him to go.

One day, without any warning,

God gave John a peek into the future!

John was not in prison on the island anymore.
He traveled to heaven in a vision.

An angel showed John many things.
John saw the holy room of God
and the throne where Jesus sits.

442

He saw the place of hell
for everyone who rejects Jesus as God's King.
He even saw Satan crushed forever!

And he also saw . . .

A new heaven and a new earth.

And then he heard something wonderful.
A loud voice came from the throne saying,
"Behold, the dwelling place of God is with man.
He will dwell with them,
and they will be his people. . . .
He will wipe away every tear from their eyes,
and death shall be no more,
neither shall there be mourning
nor crying nor pain anymore,
for the former things have passed away. . . .
I am making all things new. . . .
Write this down, for these words
are trustworthy and true."

After hearing this, John
saw a garden inside a city.
A river as clear as crystal
was flowing from the throne,
and on either side was the tree of life.

And then . . .

447

John awoke from his vision.

John smiled. John knew.

All God's promises, all the things
Jesus had told him years ago, were true!

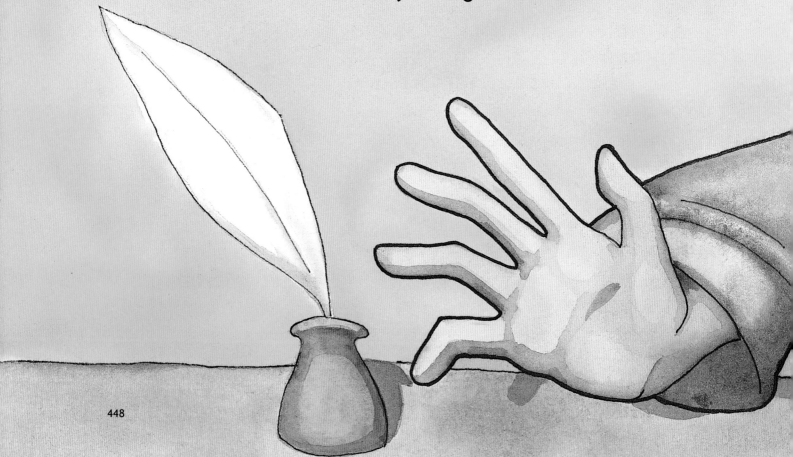

The old man could hardly write fast enough. He had seen the very good ending waiting for everyone who follows Jesus as God's King.

449

God's forever people
will one day
live in God's forever place
under God's forever rule.

451

Can you believe it?

Amen. Come, Lord Jesus!

THE **BIG PICTURE**

STORY BIBLE SERIES

Explore God's Word together as a family with *The Big Picture Story Bible* and see the big picture of God's love for you unfold from Genesis to Revelation. Teach your kids to apply God's Word with *The Big Picture Family Devotional* and help them memorize key Scripture passages with *The Big Picture Bible Verses*.

Download a free audio recording of The Big Picture Story Bible *read by the author at* BigPictureStoryBible.com